To The Green

A new
NICK W

First performance of this production
at the Donmar Warehouse
on 14 September 2000

Cast

in order of speaking

Child	DOUGRAY SCOTT
Cossum	ADRIAN SCARBOROUGH
Mo	HUGH DANCY
Duff	DANNY BABINGTON
Ain	RAY WINSTONE
Lion	NITIN GANATRA
Venus	FINBAR LYNCH
Kirkpatrick	PAUL VENABLES
Woman	JOHANNA LONSKY
Dice	DANNY SAPANI
Reconnaissance Officer	GARY POWELL

Directed by	SAM MENDES
Designed by	ANTHONY WARD
Lighting by	HOWARD HARRISON
Music by	STEPHEN WARBECK
Sound by	JOHN LEONARD *for Aura*

Company and Stage Manager	KATE CHATE
	SHARON COOPER
Deputy Stage Manager	CATRIONA STAYTE
Assistant Stage Manager	LEILA JONES
Production Manager	DOMINIC FRASER
Production Electrician	STUART CRANE
Assistant Production Manager	ALI FELLOWS
Costume Supervisor	CHRISTINE ROWLAND
Dialect Coach	JILL McCULLOUGH
Assistant Director	JOSIE ROURKE

SUPPORTED BY

The Donmar Warehouse

Since the Donmar Warehouse began life as a producing house under the artistic direction of Sam Mendes in October 1992, the theatre has asserted itself as a leader in London's performing arts community.

Deliberately embracing a diverse and daring body of work, the Donmar has created an award-winning programme that premières new work alongside bold interpretations of contemporary classics and small-scale musicals. Its commitment to producing innovative and challenging work of exceptional calibre has attracted some of the most gifted artists to its stage and has earned the theatre a worldwide reputation for excellence.

In building its repertoire over the past eight years, the Donmar has been fortunate to collaborate with some of the greatest living playwrights and composers of our time. Writers such as Alan Bennett, Brian Friel, David Hare, John Kander and Fred Ebb, David Mamet, Frank McGuinness, Peter Nichols, Harold Pinter, Sam Shepard, Stephen Sondheim and Tom Stoppard have inspired great interpretations from leading actors and directors. Together their talent has helped to build the eclectic and award-winning catalogue of work for which the Donmar has become known.

In this time, the Donmar has promoted a growing collection of new plays through its ongoing writing initiatives. Nick Whitby's *To The Green Fields Beyond* is the latest to emerge.

The Donmar Warehouse

To the Green Fields Beyond

Nick Whitby's South American trilogy of plays
premièred at the Edinburgh Festival Fringe and is still
in production across Europe. His work for Central
Television includes *Hard Cases* and *Boon*, and he has
written for various alternative comedians including
Eddie Izzard, Sean Hughes and the producers of Channel
Four's award-winning sketch show *Smack the Pony*.
He has also written a new original screenplay, entitled
Revelations, about the pioneering palaeontologist
Mary Anning.

NICK WHITBY

To the Green Fields Beyond

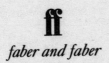

faber and faber

First published in 2000
by Faber and Faber Limited
3 Queen Square, London WC1N 3AU
Published in the United States by Faber and Faber Inc.
an affiliate of Farrar, Straus and Giroux, New York

Typeset by Country Setting, Kingsdown, Kent CT14 8ES
Printed in England by Mackays of Chatham plc, Chatham, Kent

A CIP record for this book
is available from the British Library

ISBN 0-571-20726-X

2 4 6 8 10 9 7 5 3 1

To Antony Easton
for making me write about the Great War

Sebastian Born
for his great patience and guidance

Cliff Parisi, John, Chris, Mike and Paul

. . . and the greynolds

Historical Note

The Tank Corps proper was born in February 1916, although the machine and its earliest crews were developed over the previous winter. The initial Corps of a thousand men was drawn from the Motor Machine-Gun Service, in training since late 1914. Recruits were then taken from all regiments and volunteers from the motor engineering trades. Although the initial intake was exclusively British, as the Corps dramatically expanded, men with the requisite skills were recruited from all over, including Empire regiments (among these West Indian). Some half a million men from the Indian sub-continent fought in *all* campaigns on the Allied side during the First World War.

The Tank Corps was before its time in all ways. Its chief strategist (Major J. F. C. Fuller) decribed its atmosphere as that of 'a brotherhood'. There was a belief that, if correctly used, the machine could shorten the war and bring the slaughter to an end. Liddell Hart, probably the army's most respected thinker, reported that the commanders discovered the best crews were led by, and comprised, not 'officers and men', but 'blokes'.

The tanks first saw action in September 1916, during the Somme offensive. Thirty-one of the forty-nine machines broke down before reaching the battle. In the following year (most famously at Cambrai) they made a tremendous impact, both in saving infantry lives and on the psychology of both sides. Although this remained true in 1918, when the play is set, by then the Germans had developed armour-piercing bullets, and artillery tactics that rendered the tank (with its top speed of three miles per hour) and its crew extremely vulnerable.

All Tank Corps members wore an arm-band, coloured brown, red and green. The significance of the colours to the crews is revealed towards the end of the play.

Characters

Child
Cossum
Mo
Duff
Ain
Lion
Venus
Kirkpatrick
Woman
Dice
Reconnaissance Officer

TO THE GREEN FIELDS BEYOND

ONE

The edge of a wood at dusk. France, early autumn, 1918.
As the audience enters four men are already on stage,
sitting together amongst trees. Around them are a few
blankets, some army knapsacks, respirators, a two-gallon
metal can, some shovels and lanterns. They are dressed
in oil-covered khaki overalls. They sit on logs/ground-
sheets, or rest against tree-trunks. Water is boiling in a
large pot (dixie) on a primus stove. Two of the men have
healed but heavily marked faces and skin, as if they have
been peppered with shot. One of these (Child) is writing,
the other (Venus) is mending a button on his overalls.
The other two are younger and unmarked. Mo is writing
a letter, Duff watches the stove.
Through the time it takes for the audience to come in,
the tea is poured, tin cups are handed round. When the
audience has settled, and shortly after the lights have
focused on the group, there is the crack of a snapping
twig close by. All look up. A corporal (Cossum) dressed
in regimental tunic over his overalls walks into the circle
carrying a knapsack. They all watch him dispiritedly, as
he sits with an apologetic expression.

Child No luck?

Beat.

Cossum Bogeypoke!

He suddenly jumps up, opening his knapsack,
laughing from having successfully fooled them. The
two unmarked men jump up too, clapping/whooping.

Kinch! Duckboard glide . . . Bung . . . Japan . . .

3

(*He brings out cheese, bread and a long string of black-looking sausages.*) And four pound o'mystery!

Mo Dobbs?

Cossum Dobbs, mate . . . ponks like home! Not a whiff o'stiff.

Sniffing the sausages. They all do.

Duff Where was the pigs living?

Cossum Ten mile back! Woman swore on her life.

Mo (*to Duff*) I'll have yours.

Cossum Who's babbling?

Duff holds out his hands and Cossum throws him the sausages.

Child And the other . . . ?

Cossum theatrically produces a small tube from his tunic and hands it to Child.

(*with real earnestness*) Very well done.

Duff No rabbit pie?

Cossum Duff . . . not only did I wangle you a bit o'nifty but she's got all her teeth. Near enough.

Duff Where is she then?

Cossum Hold your cock! (*to Child*) I didn't have enough after the slingers . . .

Duff Wh–at?

Cossum Wait! . . . They was ten onks . . . but I met someone. Said you knew him . . .

Child Who?

4

Cossum A ghoul. Name Kirkpatrick. Said he'd met you at Bermicourt. Anyways, he gave me the ontop, condition I brung him back here. I didn't promise him anything, said he'd have to talk with you.

Child Did he realise how close we are to the line?

Cossum He said he's been closer. Didn't stop him cacking himself when a bit of hate came over on the way up. He's got a car. He's waiting there with the nocturne, edge of the wood.

Duff Yes!

Child His own car?

Cossum Beautiful thing, American.

> *Child nods for Cossum to fetch them. Cossum goes. Two more men have appeared from the opposite direction, dressed as the others, equally marked on face and arms. The first is a lance corporal (Ain), the second ('Lion') is a Sikh and wears a turban.*

Ain I dunno which of you Cuthberts dug that but it's only on a fucking spring. There's shit floating all over . . . mainly mine 'cos my arse is peas.

Lion It's not a pretty thing to see.

> *Mo looks accusingly at Venus, who ignores everyone.*

Venus We're gone tomorrow.

Ain (*seeing the sausages*) Blimey! Mysteries! Where from? (*sniffing them suspiciously*)

Duff Ten mile back from the line.

Ain Ten mile off *this* line or the old line? Ten mile off *this* line *is* the old line.

Duff Like you're not gonna have one!

Ain I'll have one. Ey! I'm not joking you about that hole. I go buckets on the eve, and I'm not sitting ankle-high in cack, even if it's my own. Go along, lads, it's the details are important, eh? Take your Lord Lovells and dig another while it's light.

Mo (*to Child*) Can't we stay to meet the naughty?

Ain Ey?

Child (*at Mo's letter*) Finish that.

Duff And a ghoul.

Ain scrutinises them very cautiously.

Ain You're shitting me . . . ?

Duff tuts and nods in the direction the Corporal went. Ain looks that way, unable to believe his eyes, as three figures approach. He stares in wonder as Cossum, Kirkpatrick and a woman appear. Kirkpatrick is in his late thirties/early forties, dressed in civilian clothes under an army greatcoat. The woman is in her fifties.

Cossum This is Mr Kirkpatrick.

Kirkpatrick (*American accent*) Lieutenant Child . . . ? We met, sir. Last year? You don't remember me. Before Cam-brie? You wore a moustache then . . . so did I.

Child It's possible.

He turns to look at the woman who is being stared at by the men. She stands a little outside the group.

Join us.

He beckons her to approach and she steps forward a few paces.

Bon soir.

Woman Bon soir.

Child Vous êtes Belgique?

  She nods.

Parlez-vous français?

  She gestures with her hand to indicate a little.

C'est combien?

Woman Cinq francs chaque homme. Ils sont sept?

Child Huit. Il y a un autre.

  She nods, looking at the men. Ain steps forward to shake her hand . . .

Ain . . . Ain. My name. This is Duff.

  She shakes each man's hand in turn. All are very polite.

Duff Pleased to make your acquaintance.

Ain Lion . . .

  Lion bows and shakes her hand.

Venus . . .

  Venus reaches to shake her hand without getting up.

Mo . . .

Mo Honoured.

Woman Enchantée.

Child Je vous payer après. Bien?

Woman Bien. Ici?

Child Put up a blanket will you? Over there . . .

Ain Yes, sir.

The woman sits down, as Ain takes blankets and a groundsheet and starts to prepare a 'room' a little to the side.

Kirkpatrick I guess one can't be a prig on the eve of battle, eh?

Everyone looks up, at Kirkpatrick and then at Child to see how he will react.

Child Who says there's to be a battle?

Kirkpatrick Oh come on . . . There's a dozen transports come in today alone. I guess it's what you call an 'open secret'.

Child May I see your clearance papers?

He hands over some documents.

Cossum You want some char, love?

The woman looks blank.

Tea?

Woman Oui. Merci.

Lion takes his own cup, swills it out and pours her a mug of tea from the dixie.

Child You know the Brigadier General? Personally?

Kirkpatrick Spent a week at headquarters.

Child Still has Jack Russells?

Kirkpatrick (*beat*) I'm not a spy.

Child What do you want with us here?

Kirkpatrick To run a little story. From the eve of battle . . . through to the other side. Get your perspective. Your hopes and fears. That sort of thing. Make you famous. You go tonight, right?

8

Child Do you intend to write about *everything* you see?

Kirkpatrick The whole shabang.

Child Her?

Kirkpatrick Hey, there are some things I don't think my readers would appreciate. (*after a moment*) Why are you guys still two miles back from the line?

After a while . . .

Child We had mechanical trouble. We should have gone on yesterday evening. We go forward tonight. We'll be there.

Kirkpatrick Where's your tank?

Child Well covered. (*nodding towards the edge of the wood*) You ever been inside one?

Kirkpatrick No. I saw some being detrained at Erin . . .

Child Sing-song.

Lion Sahib?

Child Give Mr Kirkpatrick a tour of the car. You can ask us any questions you want. In exchange you'll take our letters, and escort our friend back.

Kirkpatrick You're a gentleman, sir.

Child (*bringing Lion back and whispering*) Don't let him touch anything. (*after him*) And tell Dice I want to know what's going on with the feed.

He moves off, followed by Kirkpatrick.

Duff Sir? What's the order? With the nock?

Child Oh . . . alphabetical I suppose.

Ain has hung the blankets up like a screen, with groundsheets spread over the ground inside forming a sort of room.

9

Ain Snug as a Paris meat-shop.

Duff A . . . B . . . Bradbeer! That's me!

Mo A for Ain.

Duff You're first up, mate.

Ain Nah, I'll go at the end. Don't want to spoil her for you.

Duff Um.

He approaches her, suddenly nervous, the others watching with amusement.

. . . Vooly-vous . . . cooshy-coo . . . avec moo . . . Siegfried Sassoon? (*gesturing towards the 'room'*)

Muffled giggles from the others. She gets up and walks towards the room, sipping her tea. Duff follows. They close the curtain behind them.

Child You two . . . (*indicating Mo and Venus*) . . . go and dig that hole.

Mo hands Child the letter he has finished. Both get up, grab shovels, and head off, leaving Cossum, Ain and Child alone. After a while . . .

Cossum How is he?

Child Same. Just sitting there, tight as a hatch. Resewing his buttons.

Ain He's quiet like he was before Hamel.

Child Not like this.

Cossum He'll perk up once he's had a pill . . . and he's emptied his apples.

Ain You got morphine?

Child produces the tube from his pocket, handing it to Ain, who starts to break up the tablets into a powder. Duff sticks his head round the curtain.

Ain What's up? Bit previous?

Duff I ain't started. (*He looks uncomfortable.*) She's got no parsley on her lemon.

The three men laugh.

Is that . . . normal?

Ain It's shaved, you mopstick, for hygiene.

Duff Oh right. I thought it might've dropped off with age . . .

They laugh more.

. . . or the needle. You certain?

Ain Use a bag.

Duff Naah. (*He goes back inside.*)

Child (*at the pills*) Let's keep that out of sight of our paperman, eh.

Ain (*at his wrist-watch*) What have you got?

Child Eight-o-five. A half should take the edge off.

Duff sticks his head out again, now half-unbuttoned.

Duff 'Nother question. Can you catch the syph off a sucky-do?

All three crack up.

Didn't think you could.

He goes back in as the three roll with laughter.

Ain (*in giggles*) ' . . . a sucky-do!' 'Can you catch the syph . . . '!

They take a while to sober up.

It's a good question. What d'you reckon?

Cossum I dunno.

Child It's a very good question.

Ain finishes crushing the pills and separating them into piles.

Ain Got a cup?

Child I'll have mine in my way. I want to be alert well before. Wake me up. You'll see to our friend . . .

They make affirmatory noises as Ain transfers some of the powder to the back of Child's hand, as Cossum pours himself a cup of tea from the dixie and holds it out to be filled. Child snorts it, Cossum and Ain drink theirs down in their tea.

Cossum What if he funks? Do we leave him behind?

Child Go across with one port gunner? I don't fancy that. Do you?

Cossum Give me his, I'm going for a word with him.

He takes the powder that Ain has done up in a twist of paper, and leaves towards the 'latrine'.
After a few moments . . .

Child I hate the night before. I've come to fear it. Fear it more than battle. (*He lets out a groan, and gets down on his knees, his forehead on the ground.*) This is . . . is very very . . . diverting. Oh God . . .

Ain puts down a groundsheet and a blanket for him to roll onto.

This is better than a sucky-do . . .

Both laugh.

Oh joy of Heaven . . . I'm asleep . . .

*Silence. Ain returns to filling his twists of paper with
the powder. We begin to hear a man's voice, singing
from the direction of the tank, and coming closer.
At the same time a grunt is heard from behind the
blankets. Dice, a Jamaican, dressed as the others with
the same marks on his face, approaches from the tank,
blowing odd notes on a bugle he's carrying and
singing. He sees the blankets up and peeks inside,
curious, then suddenly realises what he is looking
at and jumps away, with a cry.*

Dice Wa-ay! I didn't see that! (*seeing Ain*) I didn't see
that! He was jus' letting go, man, his face all twisted-up –
ugly, ugly!

Child (*dreamily, without moving or looking up*) Dice . . .
that you?

Dice Yessah!

Child You fixed the feed?

Dice Fixed good, sir.

Child Good . . . good . . .

Dice (*at the memory again*) Him going at it mash-flat
with me nanny!

*He sees the sausages cooking and sniffs them
suspiciously.*

Where the pig live?

Ain Kent. (*He holds out a twist of paper.*)

Dice No, I'm level-level. Make me belly race.

*Ain continues to hold it out until Dice takes it and
puts it in his pocket.*

Who's the bent-mouth man? (*indicating in the direction of the tank/reporter*)

Ain Ghoul.

Dice Man jump so when him see me skin. Him ask a whole ton o'question.

Ain What questions?

Dice (*thoughtfully*) All sort o'question.

Duff appears from the room, buttoning himself up.

Ain Hail the conquering hero!

Dice Look at him! All over hisself!

Ain Report.

Duff Operation successful, sah. Having softened the enemy up with a werbal barrage, and manooveering successful over the crumped terrain I was on the enemy position without delay, surprise was complete, and impressed by the sudden appearance of my engine little resistance was offered. Thereupon enfiladying her trench I emptied off both me magazines.

Through the above Mo has appeared with his shovel, and stands listening.

She mummed to give her two ticks – she's rinsing out the bag.

Ain Who's up?

Dice Not me, boy. I'm not gonna nasty up my head, an' go flabadash sheg 'pon some slack muuna, makin' four eyes with a French Lady Long Bubs Susan! 'Fore battle I take me seed with me – keep a tidy brain.

Mo Afraid she'll not have you?

Dice This is true also.

Ain I'll ask her . . .

Dice sucks his teeth to end the discussion.

Mo?

Mo starts to search his knapsack and takes out a packet of army-issue condoms.

Mo What is a Long Bub Susan?

Dice Long Bubby Susan a duppy, man, a dead woman – when she run away she throw her domplings over her shoulder go bam in your face!

Mo Yeah? Nasty. I'll watch for it.

He goes in, as Lion and Kirkpatrick approach.

Lion Char for the reporter-wallah!

Kirkpatrick looks pale and shaky, as if he has had a shock.

Kirkpatrick I'm all right, all right now . . . please . . . please . . . truly . . . (*He sits on a tree stump and takes a pull from a flask.*)

Lion It was when he went inside. Had to pull him out port sponson.

Kirkpatrick I never imagined quite . . . the smell . . .

Everyone finds this amusing.

Duff You should be there when the engine's been going all day and all four Lewises are chuckin' smoke!

Kirkpatrick . . . I can't imagine . . . can't imagine . . .

Duff We took a machine-gun crew out with us last time up. They was so sick they jumped out half way over, just sat there in no man's land, white as ghosts! And that was over flat. When it rocks there's no sailor in the fleet'd keep his breakfast down.

Kirkpatrick And you? You become used to that?

Ain We don't eat breakfast.

Kirkpatrick takes a last swig, offering the flask.

Kirkpatrick Anyone?

Ain We don't drink. Same reason.

Kirkpatrick (*at the Commander*) Asleep? There's ice? It's no work for a man with a weak stomach. It's a grim affair. Grim indeed. I noticed some of the names, at Bermicourt, they're grim too, huh? . . . You know, painted on the sides . . . ? (*Kirkpatrick takes out his notebook.*) 'Gravedigger'? . . . 'The Cynic'! But yours? 'The Time Machine.' Why?

Lion (*who has squatted down with the others, drinking tea*) It's from a story. About a man, he builds a machine, it takes him right into the future. The future's just war never-ending, and the people end up living underground. Uncanny.

Mo emerges from inside the room, doing up his buttons.

Kirkpatrick Your tank is an old Mark IV isn't it? I was told the enemy had developed weapons that could penetrate the armour on a Mark IV . . .

Ain They have.

Kirkpatrick I don't understand. Why don't you have the new Mark?

Ain 'Cos we don't want to choke to death. In the Mark V they put the radiator inside, draws the fumes in. The air goes evil. You lose your wits so you don't even have the brain to get out. We looked into a pair o' fives last up, the crews still in 'em, dead where they sat. Faces blue. We prefer to die awake. We talked it out. The eight of us.

Kirkpatrick You 'talked it out'? (*Kirkpatrick smiles and looks at the group of them.*) I was told the Tank Corps were different. I wasn't misinformed. You're an unusual . . . collection . . .

Mo We're all from different regiments. (*indicating himself*) Royal Engineers . . . (*at Ain*) Surreys . . . (*at Duff*) Essex Light . . .

Kirkpatrick What I meant was your two negroes.

Dice (*laughing, at Lion*) Ey! Him sweet-talkin' you Babu!

Ain Lion there's a pro. Punjabis, Machine-Gun Corps. Best Lewis gunner in the army. Warrior blood. Born to it. It's their religion. We only take the cream, see.

Dice The cream rise to the surface o' the churn! Eat down quick! (*Makes a long slurping noise. It goes on too long, unnerving Kirkpatrick.*)

Ain Dice is an engine man.

Kirkpatrick Really? You've had . . . training . . . ?

Dice Training!? Training you say! Me use to import motor cars cross the Caribbean. Brought 'em in in tiny pieces an' put 'em all together.

Mo What we are is talent. Each one of us can strip an engine down and put it back again, drive her and navigate her, read a map, work a radio, mend it if needs be, the lot. There's no part of our car we couldn't take a diploma in. We're a new class is what we are. The future. Technologians. Mechanicals. With the exception of Duff there, who was born to the gears on account of his being so stunted he takes up no room in the car.

Duff What!? (*pointing at Ain*) He's got class and I ain't?

17

Ain I'm number one driver on this crew, mate, on account of before all this I was a chofer . . . *a chauffeur.* Round where I'm from that's next to a fucking bishop.

Child (*in a dream or half-conscious*) . . . Snout . . . Snug . . . Flute . . . and Peter Quince . . . rude mechanicals . . . is what we are . . .

Kirkpatrick looks at them for an explanation. They shrug.

Ain I tell you what we are. We're eight bits of a machine is what we are. That's why we're still here.

He turns to see Venus and Cossum returning with shovels. He double-takes at Cossum's face, which is pale and drawn.

What's up?

Cossum gives a quick shake of the head. The moment is lost as the woman appears from behind the blankets.

Mo Thousand pardons, madamoiselle. You're up, Singalong.

Lion Not me.

Mo Venus . . . ?

Ain (*still at Cossum*) What is it?

Cossum shakes his head quickly, clearly troubled by his thoughts, grabs a blanket and curls up to sleep.

Mo Well? Who's up? The fuckstress awaits. Are you going to consult the hairy oracle?

Duff Not so hairy . . .

Venus Yeah yeah . . . (*He follows her in.*)

There is a rumble of distant explosions, no one reacts except Kirkpatrick.

Ain Black Marias. Nothing to do with us.

There is another series of explosions, coming from their other side at the same distance. At these Venus comes out from the room and stands looking in the direction of the shellfire. He listens for a while, as if for something more, and he catches the eye of Cossum, who has also sat up to listen. Ain sees the look pass between them and watches Venus turn and go, frowning, and again at Cossum, who turns away and wraps himself again in his blanket.

(at the sausages) Ey! Them dogs are barking.

Duff turns the sausages. Ain, troubled, looks at Cossum and at the sky north and south.

TWO

The focus shifts to the interior of the blanketed room, a little while on. The woman, naked under a dressing-gown, sits on the groundsheet reading from a small book. Beside her Venus is curled up asleep. She looks at her watch, closes her book, and shakes his shoulder to wake him. He wakes slowly and dreamily. He looks at her and at his surroundings. She taps her watch, apologetically. He nods, lighting a cigarette.

Venus *(making a sign)* Two minutes . . . ?

After a while she indicates the marks on his face and arms, shrugging.

Woman Comment . . . ?

Venus Spawl. Splash? The inside of a tank . . . *(She nods.)* . . . when we're hit . . . hit . . . *(He mimes someone shooting a rifle.)* . . . the metal inside . . . *(He mimes metal 'splashing' into his face.)*

She tuts sympathetically.

Woman Vous . . . ? (*She mimes someone driving.*)

Venus No. Gunner . . . (*He mimes a machine-gunner. He gets up and mimes out the positions of a tank crew in turn, giving an impression of the tight, crouched space.*) Driver . . . driver . . . gunner . . . our tank's female, yeah . . . ? No. Um . . . six-pounder male . . . our's machine-guns . . . *female* . . . two . . . in the starboard sponson . . . 'sponson'? Never mind . . . gearsman . . . ? Gears . . . to turn . . . on one side . . . starboard side . . . gearsman port side . . . port gunner . . . port gunner, me.

She nods and smiles. He smiles back.

Woman Le matin? Tomorrow?

She repeats his gunner's action. He nods, with a rueful smile.

Frighten?

After a moment he shakes his head.

Venus No. I've taken a pill. A 'pill'? (*He mimes taking a pill, then touches his heart and body indicating they are calm.*) Tomorrow . . . ? (*He indicates his heart beating fast.*) Tomorrow . . . (*He points to himself and to the crew on the other side of the blankets and draws a hand across his throat.*) Dead.

She shakes her head. He repeats the throat-cut gesture, and nods. She frowns, and makes a gesture indicating 'perhaps yes, perhaps no'. He shakes his head and then nods.

Too hard to explain. I can't explain.

She looks at him, then shows her crucifix, crossing herself and pointing to him, again with her look of inquiry.

Me? No. Sorry.

She frowns and does a long, strange mime of someone dying and their soul coming out of their body and living on next to the body. She ends it with her questioning look.

Venus I don't know what you're trying to say.

She looks at his face, wants to say something, but shrugs in frustration.

THREE

The sound of a cricket chirruping: Mo, Lion and Dice are apart from the others (Cossum, Ain, Child and Duff), who are sleeping. Empty canteens lie around, the sausages etc. having been eaten. Lion is reading haltingly from a slim book (whose title we can see is Songs of Innocence*) as the other two listen, shadow-fighting. They all speak in low voices –*

Lion
When the green woods laugh with voice of joy,
And the stream she runs laughing by,
When the air laughs with our merry wit,
And the green hill laughs with the noise of it;

When the meadows laugh with lively green,
And the grasshopper laughs in the merry scene,
When Mary and Susan and Emily
With their sweet mouths sing 'Ha Ha He!'

When the painted birds laugh in the shade,
Where our table with cherries and nuts is spread,
Come live and be merry and join with me,
To sing the sweet chorus of 'Ha Ha He!'

Silence. He turns the page, and chuckles . . .

Here is one for you, sir . . . (*He hands the open book to Dice.*)

Dice (*reading*) 'The Little Black Boy'? Ha Ha He . . .
My mother bore me in the southern wild,
And I am black, but my soul is white . . .

Is when them write this?

Mo I told you – a century ago.

Dice tuts and continues . . .

Dice
White as an angel is the English child,
But I am black, as if bereaved of light.

My mother taught me beneath a tree,
And sitting down before the day,
She took me on her lap, and kissed me,
And pointing to the east she say:

We are put on this earth but a little space
That we may learn to bear its love;
And this black body, this sunburned face,
Is but a cloud, like a shady grove.

Thus did my mother say, and kissed me;
And thus I say to little English boy.
When I from black and he from white cloud free . . .

He laughs before continuing.

When I from black and he from white cloud free . . .
And round the tent of God we joy,

I'll shade him from the heat, till he can bear
To lean in joy on our father's knee,
And then I'll stand, stroke his silver hair,
And being like him, he will then love me.

He looks at the front page of the book, thoughtfully.

Him see clear your Mr Blake – him make a good Lewis-
gunner. Still one to come . . .

*He hands the open book to Mo, as Kirkpatrick
approaches from the latrine.*

Mo Feeling any better?

Kirkpatrick A little, thank you. Haven't quite found my
stomach yet.

Mo You're lucky the shelling's been either side. Either
they don't know we're here or there's something bigger
going on north and south. You saw much infantry
coming up?

Kirkpatrick The roads were full.

Mo frowns at this.

Mo (*to Lion and Dice*) What do you make of that?

*They both look shifty, avoiding Mo's eye, shrugging
and shaking their heads.*

Kirkpatrick I don't know how you guys can sleep, you
know, before . . . ?

Mo Must be something in the cocoa.

Kirkpatrick They *are* asleep? Might I ask *you* some
questions?

They gesture him to sit.

There's one thing that's always, that I guess I've always . . .
and the public are very curious about . . . and you
understand there are many people in America of German
extraction . . . it's . . . how shall I phrase it? It's how you
actually *regard* the enemy?

Mo I never met any.

Kirkpatrick But you must have killed many?

Lion My friend, you have to understand the tank. We have been in ten battles. Twice we did not reach our starting line because of mechanical breakdown, in five we bellied before going more than two hundred yards. Only in three did we reach the enemy line.

Kirkpatrick And then?

Dice One time the enemy had left their position – fled straightway – is usual. Other time they there, their hands up, waiting there, shaking. Our commander he get out with his revolver and wait with them talking till the infantry come up. Another time they didn't surrender . . .

Kirkpatrick What happened then?

After a silence . . .

Lion Sahib. A Lewis gun fires at six hundred rounds each minute. If you reach the enemy's position and you are still receiving fire . . . you fire into that trench, all four Lewis guns at once into an area like this. That is forty bullets each and every second for twenty, thirty seconds, more. One thousand rounds of heavy ammunition at point blank. For this time the air itself turns crimson red. For some time afterwards this red cloud of . . . vapour hangs there, above, and you can smell it even from inside the tank, the blood and the flesh. You wish to write this in your newspaper?

Kirkpatrick (*beat, then casually*) Have you, or any other crew you know of, ever fired at the enemy when they were fleeing?

Silence.

It must be very hard . . . almost impossible I would say . . . in the smoke and confusion of battle, from within a tank, I mean you can hardly see at all . . . to see . . . exactly . . . ?

24

Mo (*beat*) What are you asking?

Child (*from the darkness behind*) That's enough. It's late. You're not owling it tonight, lads.

He lights a lantern. Dice and Lion get up, slinging their tea, and giving a passing shot at Kirkpatrick.

Dice You rake me *but* me riddle you. Me find me sofa. This eveling old.

Lion You been listening to gup, paper-wallah.

Kirkpatrick (*to Mo*) 'Gup'?

Mo Clack. Rumour.

Child (*from where he is still sitting, still in a dream*) You too.

Mo gets up and starts to bed down like Lion. Dice wraps himself in his blanket, takes a bugle from his bag and starts to polish it.

Kirkpatrick I meant no offence.

Child opens his eyes, staring at him. After a while . . .

Child I'll answer your questions . . . (*He nods to a place a little further away from the sleeping men.*) But quietly.

Kirkpatrick I appreciate it, sir.

Kirkpatrick takes the lantern, as Child takes a mess tin of water and joins him.

Child I'll answer your questions . . . but first you tell me what you're digging for.

Kirkpatrick I don't know what you mean.

As they talk Child washes his face and then shaves, slowly and methodically, talking in an almost dream-like way.

Child Why endanger yourself coming up here?

Kirkpatrick is unable to answer. Child smiles at him, not unpleasantly.

I never met you.

Kirkpatrick I might have been mistaken . . . mixed you up . . .

Child (*after observing him for a while*). You know, one of the peculiarities of being surrounded by danger is that a certain . . . instinct comes to the fore. Perhaps it's also to do with spending one's days in close company, and with people so 'different' from oneself. Very soon what seemed so different becomes invisible, and what is hidden clear. You are what we'd call a Holy Friar, a snarge, or a oncer. There's something 'curly' about you, two-mouthed, fly, you talk 'in your skin'. So vex me napoo samfi, open pack, don't give me rhyme an' lay me tambo, or me rax you, compree? Answer me straight and I'll be straight with you. What are you after?

Kirkpatrick I'm after the truth about this war . . .

Child Which? German? English? Civilian? Military? Newspaper truth?

Kirkpatrick Where they meet.

Child Where they meet? That will be somewhere equally offensive to all. Are you sure you're in the right job?

Kirkpatrick I've no illusions the truth may be unpopular, but this war won't go on for ever . . .

Child It won't? Oh good.

Kirkpatrick . . . And when it's over people must be told what went on.

Child And what went on?

Kirkpatrick That it didn't happen in black and white.

Child No. It's been most colourful.

Kirkpatrick That we aren't angels, the Germans devils, that our side made mistakes . . . That it was a mess . . . that the people in control weren't fit . . . that you can't run a war like a gentleman's shooting-party . . . that God wasn't 'on our side' . . . that there are things being done out here that if they were known at home the continuation of this war would become insupportable from any 'moral' standpoint.

Child And you've come to dig for such things?

Kirkpatrick I only want to tell people what this war is.

Child Wars are holy places, you know, you run the risk of being a twentieth-century sort of heretic.

Kirkpatrick I can think of few places *less* holy than a battlefield!

Child Oh, they are very very holy. Believe me.

Kirkpatrick I beg to differ . . .

Child Shut your fucking mouth and listen to what I'm saying, or I'll put my razor across your throat, we'll bury you in a hole somewhere and no one will be any wiser.

After a tense moment.

You've gone a little waxy. Got the fear of God?

Kirkpatrick You can't frighten me.

Child (*smiling pleasantly again*) That's untrue.

Kirkpatrick (*laughing nervously*) For a second I thought you were serious.

Child Did you?

He laughs with Kirkpatrick, whose laughter dries up.

No, dear chap, the truth is I've got nothing against you, in fact the reverse, and you are perfectly right, there is more to this war than people are aware of, and I'll not pass up the opportunity of sharing it with you.

Venus suddenly emerges from the room.

Set fair?

Venus What's the time?

Child Three hours yet. Fetch some sleep.

Venus (*nodding inside*) I have. I'll bitch her some tea. Poor mad-mozzle's dead on her pratt.

Child You want the truth about this war? (*Kirkpatrick indicates a yes.*) The truth is too big for a newspaper column. Even if you got it you'd have to chop it into something false to fit.

Kirkpatrick That's why I need something, some . . . 'image' . . . that shows the great lie.

Child Do you know the biggest lie of this war? Blame. The searching for blame. That's what lays me low, that out of it, people like you won't make the effort to understand its meaning, but in your ignorance find no more than something or somebody to *blame*. (*after a moment*) Which war are you interested in?

Kirkpatrick I don't understand.

Child There have been two wars in this war. The first . . . a war of mud . . . and innocence . . . disillusion . . . and a second war. It was born as the first shot was fired till now there isn't any other. It is to coin the phrase 'futureistic'. This is the war we are in, and I fear, emotion being stronger than truth, the pedlars of simplicity will ensure the first will be remembered, while this one, the important one, will not. You're after an 'image' . . . (*Beat.*) At

Boulogne . . . when we got off the boat this tour, on the docks there were umpty porters, Africans, Orientals and others I couldn't tell. They were unloading crates . . . supply crates . . . full of food, ammunition, fodder, what have you. They'd stacked them up in three pyramids, each one the size of a cathedral. I asked the sergeant there who it was all for. He said a division – just one of a hundred like it in the army. They were *one week's supplies. One* week. For one division. On the very top of one I remember a Chinaman smoking a pipe . . . strangest thing. In the morning the pyramids were gone. They were building another.

Kirkpatrick Armies must be fed.

Child 'A *mess*?' You think this war was *under-planned*. Let's crack open one of those cases . . . one . . . and take out a shell. A high explosive shell, be careful. Unscrew the timing cap . . . just one shell in millions . . . what's there? Twenty-two separate pieces of tooled brass. Like a fob-watch. Each piece machined to within a fraction of an inch, put together just so to make the timer balance, by hand, just so. The craft of it! The precision, the love and care that goes into it . . .

Venus passes Child a cup of tea and sits listening.

. . . into chaos. It is enantiodromia.

Kirkpatrick Excuse me?

Child Pardon my education. It's Greek. For a time when everything meets its opposite. An Apocalypse. The 'unveiling' . . . an unveiling of the truth. I told you, this is a holy place . . .

Kirkpatrick (*dubiously*) Go on . . .

Child Heaven and Hell, real, here, now, created on earth . . . anywhere that isn't the Hell two miles up there is a little Heaven. Day is become night, night day . . . the living *living* amongst the dead, angels and devils *flying* in the air above, *flying*! North meets south, east meets west . . . for the first time in the history of mankind all the colours and races of the world brought together *in one place.*

Cossum (*from the shadows*) ' . . . and there before me was a fourth beast – terrifying and powerful. It had large iron teeth; it crushed and devoured its victims, and trampled what was left beneath it.' Book of Daniel.

Kirkpatrick I'm not a religious man . . .

Child Neither am I! Neither am I, but when life becomes this ugly, there must be something equal of beauty hiding within. A great truth. Don't you think so? We are at the gates of a better world. That is what I believe.

   Dice comes forward. He has his bugle, that he
   continues to clean with a rag.

Kirkpatrick Look, you must fight tomorrow, I'll not argue with you. But if you say this war is the Last War, and prophesied in the Bible, I do not believe it.

Dice Tell the man the calc'lation.

Cossum 'From the beginning to the beginning of the end will be one thousand two hundred and ninety days. Blessed is the one who waits till the end of one thousand three hundred and thirty-five days.' Black and white. In the Holy Lands the war against the Turk began in March '15. It says the final battle will begin one thousand two hundred and ninety days after, that's now, the middle of September '18. The battle will last forty-five days, till the beginning of November. That's when the war will end.

Kirkpatrick November this year? No chance!

Cossum I'd a letter from a mate in Palestine. In the 135th Emma-Gees – bivvied down outside a town called Megido. Our name for it is Armageddon. That's what it's called in The Book. They're set up there for the final push against the Turk. Tanks and cavalry forming up behind, for a great charge through Arma-fucking-geddon. This war's over after that, and there's gonna be peace, and it's gonna last for ever. For-ever-and-ever.

Dice blows his bugle.

Kirkpatrick You all believe this?

Cossum I do.

Dice An' I.

Venus shrugs.

Kirkpatrick (*to Child*) You? (*mockingly*) And you say you're not religious . . .

Child This war has opened me up. You say this isn't a war of black and white. Your whole reality is black and white. Things are happening, *extra-ordinary* things. You awake, Mo?

After a moment.

Mo Yeah.

Child Tell him about your German.

Kirkpatrick German?

Mo Bert One-Stone.

Child He had a very different idea of reality.

Kirkpatrick He was . . . your prisoner?

Child Prisoner? Now why do you say that?

Kirkpatrick looks uneasy as Child stares at him through the following.

Mo Bert One-Stone's a scientist. A German. Two years ago, on the eve of the Somme, he published his theory.

Cossum Not this again!

Mo In it he said that what we took as the truth wasn't truth at all. He showed it with equations. But what it amounted to was so hard to understand that even when you understand it you won't credit it. He showed the reality behind reality is from *all* perspectives. And when you try to grasp it, the mind being singular, you can't keep hold of it. Can't image it. It slips away. Like a vision, there and gone.

Kirkpatrick is still uncomfortably aware of Child staring at him.

And very beautiful.

Kirkpatrick Really?

Child (*to Kirkpatrick*) I know why you're here.

Mo He showed things that cut so deep in time and space they make the Prophets of Old seem like children drawing pictures in the sand . . .

Cossum That's a matter of opinion.

Mo Yeah, the right one. He proved other things too. That matter . . . this (*picking up the dirt*) . . . is just *energy*, temporarily locked up, an emission of trapped nothing. A belch . . . ! More . . .

Cossum Somebody sit on him . . . !

Dice It's this type o'talk is my objection to the university-style education!

Dice comes up behind Mo and stuffs his armband in his mouth to shut him up, holding his arms to prevent him taking it out. It is playful and routine.

Mo More . . . ! There's more . . . there's more . . . (*etc., until silenced*)

Dice No there is not . . . (*etc., gagging him*)

Mo is stopped from continuing . . . ('That's just the beginning . . . Time itself, Time itself! . . . is made up of . . . ')

Kirkpatrick If what this man said is so significant I think I might have read about it.

Venus Hey, Mo, so what, tomorrow you're lying there all shot up on a stretcher, breathing your last . . . and you're there, and the doctor's bent over you at your last gasp . . . and he's going, 'Who do you want . . . a chaplain . . . a priest?' (*as a dying man*) . . . 'No, no . . . bring me . . . an academic!'

Laughter as Mo manages to wriggle an arm free, remove his gag, and continue, warding off Dice's attempts to replace it.

Mo Why should you have read about it? The press deals in news. What's news? Something that didn't happen yesterday, and matters less tomorrow. If Jesus-call-me-Christ came down and gave a sermon on a Monday, it wouldn't even get a mention in the Fridays. And what if the truth is the only truth's to look at things from infinite perspectives? Try selling that to your editor. (*not flashpoint*) Get off! (*Dice gives up.*)

Kirkpatrick I'm only doing what you say, attempting to show another point of view.

Child Your story's already written, all you're after is the topline. This war won't open you. Until you've sunk into this war, until you've . . . (*He stops himself.*) You cannot see what we see, you cannot know what we know. That's not your fault. What is your fault is that you've come here to judge us.

Kirkpatrick I'm not judging anyone . . .

Child I *know* what you're after!

Kirkpatrick I truly don't know what you mean.

Child Liar. (*He stares at him.*) Tell them why you're here!

Kirkpatrick I'm here to understand this war, that's all!

Child That it? (*He takes the razor from his pocket, and opens it.*) Well I can help, I can help!

He grabs Kirkpatrick, forces him to the ground and, straddling his arms, puts the razor to his neck. Everyone reacts as Kirkpatrick screams.

(*to Dice, Venus and Cossum, who all jump up*) Stay where you are!

Cossum (*to Dice, at Ain*) Wake him!

Child (*to Kirkpatrick*) Is this what you were after? Yes? Yes? (*He does something unseen with the razor as Ain is shaken awake by Dice.*) There!

The woman has emerged to see what is happening as Child gets up, leaving Kirkpatrick clutching at his neck and seeing blood on his hands.

Kirkpatrick (*in stunned horror*) What have you done? You've killed me.

Child (*cleaning his razor*) I took a nitch out of your ear. You have the smallest wound of the war.

Those watching laugh out of relief. Lion has woken at the cries.

34

I could even it up if you like?

Ain (*coming forward*) That's enough . . .

Kirkpatrick He attacked me, for no reason . . .

Child Ask him why he's here.

Ain Ey, enough enough!

> *As Child goes for him again, Ain grabs him round the middle, pinning his arms.*

Easy . . . easy . . . easy . . .

> *Child continues to struggle, trying to get at Kirkpatrick with the razor.*

Be good, be good . . .

Child Let go!

Ain Not till you're velvet . . .

Child That was an order . . .

Ain And I don't give a fuck, old pot . . . not till you're kiff . . .

Child I'm kiff.

Ain What you want to cut his tab for, eh?

Child I know why he's here . . .

Kirkpatrick He keeps saying that!

Ain We've got work tomorrow. This ain't the night to go winnick, matey . . .

Child We won't get another.

> *Silence.*

You know what I'm talking about.

Ain (*quietly in Child's ear, aware of the others*) Ssh. Now chub it.

Child . . . You know what I'm saying . . .

Ain (*whispered*) Stop your mouth.

This quietens Child.

What's the matter with you, eh? You need releasing?
Well there's a bit of soft standing there who, I grant
you, may be past her monthlies, and have a pair of top
bollocks like two socks on a washline, but she's still the
most lovely thing you'll ever ever see. Her eternity box
awaits your dearly beloved, and she'll wonder if she's
losing her charms if you don't pop it in. Would you want
that on your conscience?

Child cannot help smiling and relaxing.

Tie and blazer.

*Child opens the palm of his hand. Ain takes the razor
and releases him. Child straightens himself out and
walks into the room. She follows. After a while . . .*

Ain Dice, take him to the car and patch his tab.

Kirkpatrick I've heard of men court-martialled for less
than you've just done.

Ain Yeah, well . . . we're different, aren't we? We're
from another time, mate. You ain't got that yet, have
you?

Kirkpatrick follows Dice towards the tank.

Venus How long till the Contour's here?

*Ain checks his wrist-watches, and starts rooting in his
knapsack for toilet paper.*

Ain While yet. Touch of the umptyiddies? Have a shit.

Venus shakes his head.

Your arse be it. Singsong . . . Joey . . . Corp? (*with
hidden meaning*) Keep it bonzer, eh?

*Lion, Venus and Cossum all acknowledge this, seen
by Mo, as Ain goes.*

Mo What did he mean by that?

Cossum San fairy ann.

After a moment.

Mo I know there's something up.

There is an uneasy silence amongst the other three.

Duff? Duff! He's asleep. You think we'll funk because
we're novvies?

Cossum There's nothing up.

Mo You know something.

Silence.

Cossum We don't know anything.

Mo What is it?

All three avoid his eye.

Is it my imagination is it . . . everybody's out of curl?
The Chief's gone dis like that before then, has he? (*at
Venus*) You in a wet flipping trance all day, you both and
Dice with Friday faces on? You think I don't see? Last
two outings weren't like this. What was the name of that
place . . .

Lion Buquoy.

Mo We had a bloody singsong. Eh? Now what's going
on, you telling me I'm green? What was that look there?!
I thought there weren't any secrets with us!

After a while . . .

Cossum Mo. Look mate . . . look . . . it's nothing.
There's nothing.

37

Mo You swear that on your God?

Silence.

It's you has got the morbs! You're shamed you've got the breeze in front of me and Duff! Ha! That's what this has been about. It's gone round you like the needle and we didn't click! That's it, isn't it!? It's the quietness has got to you. You're not used to it, are you?

Silence.

You're not used to a night before with no shelling, waiting back like this with no hate coming over.

Ain returns from the side, and stands listening.

It's too peaceful for you. That's all it is. Isn't it? That's all it is. That's all it is.

Cossum You know what it is. Don't you?

The good humour visibly drains from Mo's demeanour.

Mo They're waiting for us, aren't they? That's why nothing's come over. Tell me.

Lion And me. I was not sure.

Venus Have you ever seen a sky so filled with obbos as it was today? And not one shell come over?

Child comes out hurriedly, having heard Venus begin his explanation.

Not one shell. Listen to it.

They listen to the silence.

They know the tanks are here. They've brought their big stuff up. They want us to come on. Tomorrow we'll roll into it, bobbing drill, our armour will be as good as cotton. We're spendable. (*to Lion*) Pig meat.

Lion . . . Suar ka maas.

Venus Dead men.

Mo You can't be certain.

Venus What other reason? They've chucked it over north and south . . . but not here. There must be near two hundred tanks in this eight mile. You think they wouldn't even crump the ground to slow us down? Believe me, friend, after three years you can read a night-before, clear as words on paper. When we go across they'll have enough Fairy Lights to day the night, and half-a-dozen field guns trained on each and every tank. We're in the knackers' yard, friend, don't pull the wool.

Mo looks to the others, whose faces concur.

Child Perhaps if something had come over, an hour ago . . . even now . . .

They wait, listening.

But it isn't coming.

After a while.

Mo You all suspected it, but didn't say . . . ? Dice too?

Lion He knows.

Mo (*at Duff under his blanket*) And Duff?

Lion I don't see that he should know.

Child I agree. Where ignorance is bliss.

Ain He won't funk it . . .

Cossum He should know.

Child Why must he?

Cossum 'Cos we're crew.

Child Show hands. Ay . . . ?

Cossum and Ain put up their hands.

. . . Nay?

Child and Lion raise theirs.

Joey . . . Mo?

Mo I can't call . . .

Venus . . . No, nor I.

Child Then it's Dice's vote.

Lion Tch. That cannot be.

Child He must have his vote.

Lion That will make it his decision alone. That is not democracy.

Cossum Singsong, you ignorant demi-coon, democracy *means* one man one vote.

Lion Corporal, with great respect, you shit for brains, democracy is not so simple. If he was here with us when we show hands, then it would *be* democracy, but what we are doing now is pass the vote *to* him. That is *casting* vote. In his heart the responsibility then will have been his, and his alone. And that is not fair.

Cossum Tell him!

Child He's right.

Beat.

Cossum Cunt.

Lion Your apology is accepted.

Chastened silence.

Child Can we come to an agreement? Do we tell him?

Ain We're forgetting it's Duff here. He don't have the necessary intellects to funk it. This is the 'erb who wore his respirator upside-down through Hamel, who reckons Paris is the capital of Germany. But he's a bloke who's happier in this crew than he's been in his whole fucking life, and he wouldn't lose it in front of us if it gave him life eternal. He's been lying there for the last ten minute crying his heart out.

Duff (*without moving*) No I ain't! I'm ready.

Venus I'm not. I haven't got the breeze, but this one isn't necessary. Is it?

Child What isn't?

Venus Anything could go wrong, couldn't it? Between here and the jump-off.

He looks at the faces now all looking at him.

We could break a track. Belly her on a tree-stump.

Cossum Careful.

Venus We've done our job. We've pulled in all their heavy stuff. We won't make one blind bit of difference tomorrow, not to anything. Why kill ourselves san fairy ann?

Silence.

All of you have thought it. I only said it. Don't look at me.

Child Yeah, you said it. You've crossed the line, Joe.

Venus What's the line?

Child You know what I'm talking about. The rule that says I don't brass, the rule that says there are no rules, except we do our job. The thing that makes us different . . . that keeps a bit of something alive . . .

41

Venus So we can just chuck it away? Yeah, everything can be discussed. Everything but this! The important thing.

Child You want to discuss it?

Ain We ain't got the time.

Child We've time . . .

Venus And if we're split, like we were just now, what then?

Child We'll sit down and talk this through, in our way. A majority says go, we go. Ditch her, and we ditch her. Who's still for the nock?

Cossum Me.

Ain . . . And me.

Child Get on with it then.

Ain nods Cossum to go first. Cossum enters the room. Dice approaches with Kirkpatrick, his ear dressed and wearing his respirator.

What's wrong with him?

NB: for a while there's been a faint smell of burnt almonds mixed with cordite in the air.

Dice (*amused*) He caught a smell o'gas.

Child It's only on the air, from the north. It won't hurt you, take it off.

Kirkpatrick shakes his head. Dice looks round at everyone's face . . .

Dice Wha' brok?

Lion There's no secrets no more.

Dice reacts to this, showing he understands.

42

Child We're going to talk it out. Talk it out no differently than if it were the machine, and she'd just rattled and choked. Let's look at our chances of coming through, weigh them and the options if we decide against. Let's look at everything.

Venus We're doing this in front of *him*? (*indicating Kirkpatrick*) What *if* we decide against?!

> *Silence, as they all stare at the increasingly nervous-looking Kirkpatrick.*

Child Take off the fucking mask!

> *He does so.*

If we slip this battle what will we do with you, do you think? This is your last chance. You still pretending we don't understand each other? Tell them. Tell them why you're here! Be honest and I'll let you go.

> *After a moment.*

Kirkpatrick I don't know what you mean.

Child Tie him up.

> *They start to do so.*

Kirkpatrick You can't do this . . . you can't do this . . . !

Child You had your chance.

Kirkpatrick What's going to happen to me?

Child Stick that back on him!

> *They put the mask back on, shutting him up, and sit him back down on the ground.*

(*at Kirkpatrick's terrified eyes*) You'd better pray *we're* honest. (*to the others*) Are we agreed, whatever we decide, whichever way, is binding on us all?

> *Everyone nods, agrees.*

43

Let's make it formal then. (*at his wristwatch*) Midnight here. Singsong . . . do your magic with a fire.

He indicates a place in the centre for a fire to be lit, and then crouches close by to write a letter. Lion picks up a handful of twigs and crouches down. Several pull logs up round the fire, sitting, watching in silence as he arranges it with extreme simplicity, catches some matches thrown to him, and lights it. The fire takes. Through the above, as almost everyone's attention is taken up with the fire, Cossum slips unnoticed out of the room. He looks slightly bemused, looks around and sees that Dice is doing something with his knapsack, slightly apart from the others.

Cossum (*quietly, so as not to draw attention*) Hey, Dice . . .

Dice What?

Cossum gestures him over, away from the others, so that no one can hear them.

Wha' mek?

Cossum There's something funny with her.

Dice The nookoo? Too ripe she for you?

Cossum No, no . . .

Dice What then?

Cossum I took me overs off, right, and got it out . . . (*He makes a masturbatory gesture with his closed fist.*) . . . jub jub, right?

Dice Uh.

Cossum . . . and shot me me jelly into my hand . . . and went to rub it on her oojimaflip, and she pushed my

44

hand away, made like I was doing it wrong. But I wasn't. I wasn't . . . was I?

Dice stares at him, open-mouthed for a second, then covers it. He stares at Cossum, lost between feelings of astonishment and pity.

Was I?

Dice (*beat*) No man, no. You by the book.

Cossum Right.

He joins the others round the fire, leaving Dice too stunned to move. He stares at Cossum who has quietly taken a place around the fire.

Lion (*seeing Dice crouching down, head in hand*) What's up with you?

Some of the others turn to look.

Dice My head go dizzy, feel like I gonna fene.

Child You had some powder?

Dice Nah man. Somethin' unexpected stuck in my throat.

Lion What is stuck?

Dice Nothing. It go down.

The others return to the fire.
  After a while Dice gets up, wiping his eyes, unseen, and quietly joins the others around the fire.
  Lights fade down on the group.

FOUR

Inside the room. The woman is alone. Ain enters. She gestures him towards the groundsheet where she's lying.

Ain Um . . . No. I'm not . . . (*He takes out and shows her a photograph.*) My wife. Five minutes . . . sank minutes here . . . okay? I don't want no one thinking I'm superior. Tch. You don't compree. I don't parly love . . .

Woman (*in English as though speaking Flemish*) Do you want to stay? Don't worry, I'll be paid anyway.

Ain Tch. How to make you understand. Sank minutes. Sank eecee?

Woman Okay. San fairy ann?

Ain (*laughing, relieved she understands*) San fairy ann!

She gestures him to sit. He does so.

. . . Don't stop talking. I don't know what you're saying but don't stop . . . I wish I could tell you what's in here . . . (*indicating his head. He looks at her questioning expression. After a moment*) I'm scared I'll mess myself. Last four times up, waiting for the go, I've messed myself. I can't help it. It don't matter if there's nothing in me, I just . . . I never used to. The chief knows, he *must* know, but the others don't know, maybe they know . . . parly to me, parly vous . . .

Woman I talk? Is that what you want?

Ain . . . parly . . .

Woman I am tired. You've a face older than its years, like mine . . . I can read faces, you know. In four years I have seen ten thousand faces, more . . . if I think . . . of seven men each day. I can read faces, each detail, and

46

then they're gone . . . (*with a gesture indicating from her memory*) I have served the British army for four years . . . I left Belgium when it began. Life is very strange. This war has brought me peace. In here . . . (*touching her heart*) I did not have it before. I do not think my country will give me a medal. It doesn't matter. I'll tell you the truth? I am proud of what I do. If I miss a day I feel . . . bad. So many must have died within days of coming to me. Life can be stranger than the strangest things you can imagine. What is dark may be light, what is meaningless may become the truth . . . what is ugly can be beautiful. Do you think this war will make a world that understands such things?

Silence.

I'm glad you can't understand me.

Silence.

Frighten? You?

Ain Me? Normal frightened for a night before. I drive . . . (*He mimes moving two levers*) . . . drive? They believe in me, y'see? So I put a mask on it. Mask. Like you, love.

He smiles at her. She shrugs, then returns it.

FIVE

The crew are seated (on blankets/logs, etc.) in silence in a crescent around the small fire. Kirkpatrick is still tied, wearing the mask. Ain comes out from the room and joins the circle.

After a silence . . .

Child So. Let's not spare anyone's feelings. Open pack. (*to Venus, at Mo and Duff*) In case anyone's not clear. Lay out what we're rolling into.

47

Venus Well it's gonna be short. If his heavy stuff's dug in forward we're not gonna get far. Let's say just one of his seven-sevens picks us out . . . two bracket shots, he'll get us third or fourth shot. That's a minute, maybe two if we're lucky. Unless we spot him, but that's wishing. Take your memory of all the battles you've been in, press them into sixty seconds and end it with one head-fucking bang. It'll be short. That's the best to say for it.

Child Anything to add?

Silence. Some shake their heads.

Lion I have. I think this discussion is improper. A soldier's duty is to fight. Only that. To do what he is told. Like the tracks of our machine, we go round. We serve. No more. To question it is a kind of madness.

Venus Not to question our position is madness. I'm not saying we duck our duty, I am saying we duck *this* fight, and fight another day. Why waste ourselves?! Three years we've come, three years, to be here!

Lion The other crews in our section will look to their left and right and see we are not there. Picture *them*. Yourself as *them*.

Venus I don't need to imagine, I remember Flers when we were the only ones to make the starting line. Who knows why the others didn't make it?

Lion I tell you, it is preservation of yourself that is at the heart of your arguments. Without it you would not be making them.

Venus eyeballs him. There is palpable tension.

Venus What?

Lion You heard me . . .

48

Dice Cho! Easy. If you warify me cross-cut you fore it turn into a licking-match! Take the moral of the thing away, the moral bring only war.

Venus You think what I'm saying's just the breeze?!

Ain Ey, Joey, you're no coward. (*to Lion*) You remember Arras, mate.

Silence. Child sees Mo *and* Duff *frowning, wanting to know.*

Child Tell *them*.

Ain We over-heated . . . fifty yards from their line, it can't've been no more, we'd had an APB come in and pip the radiator, we hadn't seen, the smoke lifting, and we were sat there like a stuck cow, the engine seizing up, and he jumps out the door and he's fetching water in his mask from a shell-hole!

Venus Then it was do something or sit there and get hit – there was nothing else. But this is different, 'cos there *is* something we can do, and yes, I am justifying it, 'cos I want a way out of this.

Silence.

If we don't use our brains we're not coming out. I can't swallow having come this far to just walk into this. It's not what we're about. We're special. Always have been, since the start, since Dice and you (*Lion*) turned up. (*at Child*) On account of you and your socialisumistic shit we've always done things open. I fucking laughed at you at the beginning, but the fact is we're still going when most of them we trained with are landowners. Has that been luck? I don't know, but I do know a lot of them squires of the six-by-two went into battle scared of each other, eight stiffs in a tin box, when we went in laughing . . . a crew. But we're not laughing tonight.

49

And we're not a crew. I don't go for any of that spiritual mumbo, but there's times when I could swear there's been something protecting us. And I'll say it now, I'll say it, 'cos the truth's always been our way . . . I don't feel it tonight.

Silence.

Child We've all felt it.

Mo Us too.

Duff We felt it since we first came on. From the start.

Mo And you're right, it isn't here tonight.

Silence.

Ain Hey . . . (*at his watch*) We'd better move this on.

Dice I tell you what it is give me iniquity. Maybe this is why the Lion talk so farad . . . but I tell you, if we belly the machine and we no fight, *after*, *after* when a man look into me eye an' beg me swear if it were for real . . . ? He want to see the lie, he see the lie. Me have me nation to think about.

Lion I hear.

Mo I hear you too. You can't fuck with your conscience if you're a wog. Speaking as a white one.

Lion I apologise. I spoke jildi.

Venus That's alright, you're a cunt.

Lion Thank you.

Cossum This 'something protecting us'. Your words. I believe in it. In angels.

Venus Oh we are fucked!

Cossum (*talking over*) . . . And if we have one, if we do, I don't reckon we ought to tick it off by talking about ditching the machine.

Venus It's something we're putting out, that's all! Just wishing!

Cossum No. No. (*to Mo and Duff*) After Wipers, when you first came on board, and you were on divvy, you used to put nine rations out. Three, four times you did it, you remember that? *They* didn't know. And there were other times. But it started after Wipers. Am I doolally-tap?

Ain You ain't doolally . . .

Dice . . . Me an' him we talk on it aback.

Mo What are you on about?

Child It was at Wipers we lost the two men you replaced.

Duff We said we'd never ask . . . unless you spoke it first.

Mo What happened?

Ain We haven't time for this . . .

Child We've time.

Ain He's gonna come and we're still sitting, talking . . .

Child There's time. Go on.

Mo What happened to them? How did they die?

Child Hart died, Brown's still alive. (*He looks to Ain to tell.*)

Ain Day before the off at Wipers, we were in a line of cars going up to the starting line, on a raised road we were, off the swamp. A hail o'hate came over, big stuff, a lot of H.E. We got pitched off down the bankment into the filth. Most of us broke something, but we all walked out of it. 'Cept for Hart and Brown. They was in the starboard sponson we'd come down on. The engine block 'd sheered off from the frame and come down on 'em inside. We got Mickey out, Mickey Brown . . . bottom half of his face was in a shocking state . . . just flat . . . but Hart was stuck there, under the block. He was alright, but stuck. Ah, fuck . . .

Cossum It began to rain.

Lion . . . like a monsoon rain . . .

Mo (*beat*) You don't have to tell us . . .

Cossum He didn't drown.

After a moment.

Dice The man was rhymin', all through the water rise. He never black up, for true, even when only him chin' an' neck long out the filth.

Cossum The mud was so thick we couldn't pump it out, and the ground so crumped we couldn't get a crane in. On the third morning we'd given up. No one said nothing but he knew. We fed him his breakfast, talked, (*to Ain*) you took down the letter to his mum and dad . . . then about four or five o'clock he just gave it up. Went so easy. So easy it was weird. It's made me think he went so easy . . . maybe he never went so far.

Venus Hang up, hang up . . . we're ranging way off the target here . . .

Cossum Are we? I don't think so. When I saw him pass I thought, that's how to go. He went so clean. I want to go with my conscience clean like that.

Dice I hear.

Venus You've both got trumpets in your ears. Last fucking battle! Yeah, and all men will be brothers, well the whole Bible kicked off with a pair of brothers, didn't it? They weren't too bloody civil!

Cossum This is why the spirit's gone. We're split. When we were tight the spirit was around. Perhaps he doesn't want to come round us now . . .

Venus Shit! Am I the only sane man here!? I don't feel his ghost! Nor did you, any of you, till you just conjured it!

Cossum You said you felt something protecting us . . . a spirit, *you* said!

Venus Coming out of *us*! *May be*! *May be*! I don't know how else we're all still here, but it comes from *us*. And if we do go into battle, and if you go *I go*, I don't care what it is or where it's from but we'd better fucking find it. We'd better find it quick. That's all. I've had my say.

Silence.

Ain (*muttering*) Come on . . . come on . . .

Child I make that three on one. Duff . . . Mo?

Mo Correct me if I had it wrong. I understood we won't be coming out of this. I'm scientific by training, I like to have things set out so they're clear. What we are choosing here, in simple terms, is life or death. That choice is an easy one for me.

It passes to Duff.

Duff I don't have no problem here. I'm Roman Catholic. I can't choose the road to self-destruction. It's immortal sin.

Cossum What you join the fucking army for?

Duff Birds, mate.

Cossum Birds?

Duff Yeah. My neighbour said if I joined she'd let me cop her muffin.

Child And did you? Cop her muffin?

Duff Not to date.

Child Why?

Duff I've only had Christmas leave, haven't I? Too nippy.

After laughter from the others.

(*at Mo who is staring at him*) What . . . ?

Mo You're not a Catholic.

Duff I could be.

Cossum Ey, this ain't the time to fuck about, matey.

Duff I beg to differ, matey.

Silence.

The lot of you've gone heavy.

Ain Duff.

Duff What?

Ain You're a cunt supreme.

Duff You genuine?

Ain Yeah.

Duff (*genuinely*) Ta.

Dice You wiser than you short, boy.

Duff smiles to himself.

Child So what's your call?

Duff Eh? Life.

Child Else?

Ain takes a long, deep breath before starting.

54

Ain I've got to drive the fucker in, lads. This last week I locked off my mind. Now I've gotta think with it . . . shit!

Dice Come on, man . . .

Ain If we cut this fight, I know one thing, we'll pay for it. None of us should cod himself. We'll pay. I don't know what pain can be, real pain. I've had a share. I don't know what it is to live without your arms, or a face, or only half a brain. I don't know what it is to die, or be dead. Maybe the imagining of it is the worst of all. I don't know. I know something though. This is where pain happens. (*indicating his head*) Nowhere else. There is no pain without this thing up here, no Hell like mental Hell, and no torture like what a man can afflict on himself. In here. If we cut this thing, if we do, from tonight each and every one of us will have it run in his head, for the remains of his life, like a ghost, like a dream you can't wake from, in his imagining, real as day, till his last breath.

  Silence.

More . . . if we cut . . . if we do, then every time we've ever had together, everything we've ever known . . . the moments . . . we've done, shared, had . . . every scrap of comfort we've ever taken out of this . . . is made into something else . . . napoo . . . gone. (*after a moment*) That's all shit. I'll tell you what I feel, I'll tell you what I *feel*. You've got some fucking metal, mate, (*at Joe*) 'cos what you said is courage. Pure. And if this was about metal, like we know it, metal, where it matters . . . being where it *matters* . . . there wouldn't be no choice, we'd slip this fight. We'd slip this one, die some other night.

  Venus cries openly. He cries from relief, as if some great weight has lifted.

But there's more . . . something bigger though come out this war, for *me*, than either living or dying. That's us. Not each of us. Just us. When we click I don't have no fear, of *nothing*. It must be a thousand times I've put my life in your call, you in mine, it never even crossed my mind to think. The fact that you're a bag of buckles, wogs and country inbreds is . . . is a freak of nature's what it is. It's something . . . bigger than this war . . . like a kingdom come. It fills me with pride, and hope, and love. It fills me with love.

Silence.

I'm not gonna make no choice, one way or other, 'cos for me the choice ain't it. I'll drive you, I'll *follow* you, whatever way you go, but let's do it in one mind and one heart. No one dragging, no regret, no one hung up . . . together. Then I'll face anything. (*after a while. He turns to Child.*) Sorry, Chief. Your call.

Child This must be my fate. No man in this war wanted less to be an officer than me. I'm normal, lads, I'm just a schoolteacher, and you're not children. I feel the same now as I've always felt. You've stuck fast to your beliefs. I'm no different. I'll stick to mine. I won't make this decision for another man, and not for you.

Lion You won't make it?

Child I won't make it.

Mo Now we're bellied.

Venus What do we do?

Child We put it to a higher power.

Cossum You don't believe in no higher power.

Child Chance.

Venus You put that higher than reason?

56

Cossum Or duty?

Child That settles it.

Venus/Cossum What/What does?

Child It must be fair since both of you object. (*to Dice*) Give me your bones!

Dice hands him some dice.

Six says we go.

Cossum That's not right . . . that's odds of one in six!

Child Six throws. If it's meant, it's meant. (*He looks at each in turn.*) We stick to it. Body and mind, heart and soul.

Dice Mind, body, heart and soul.

Lion nods, followed by Cossum.

Child Say it.

Venus/Mo/Duff Mind, body, heart and soul.

Child (*giving the die to Lion*) You throw. The six of you.

Someone puts down a mess tin in the middle for them to throw it into. Lion throws. They watch as it rolls and stops, clearly not on a six by the reactions. Dice, as the next, steps forward, picks it up and rolls it. The same result. Cossum does the same. Mo comes forward and picks it up, more hesitantly . . .

Cossum Roll it . . . roll it!

Mo does so. The tension building, some watching, some unable to . . . it stops. They look. Duff steps forward and takes his turn. Same result.

Child Last roll, Joe . . .

Venus picks up the die, taking his time, blowing on it for luck.

Cossum Odds are stacked against you now, mate . . .

Mo They're the same.

Cossum It's not come up five times.

Mo It's still one in six.

Venus Yeah? That doesn't make sense.

Mo Numbers don't.

Venus Maybe there's something in the air, doesn't want it to come up, eh?

Lion/Cossum Roll/Roll it . . . roll it! . . .

As Venus shakes the die, Ain's attention is drawn to something beyond the trees. There is the faint sound of men's voices, singing.

Ain Shh!

Child gestures to Venus to hold his throw. They all turn, listening. It is a marching song, sung slow to a marching rhythm by many voices, like a great low hum. It comes closer, passing the edge of the wood where the tank is . . .

Voices Singing
Rolling on . . . rolling on . . . rolling on . . . rolling on . . .
By the light of the silvery moon,
Rolling on . . . rolling on . . . rolling on . . . rolling on . . .

Everyone stops to watch a hundred flickering cigarette ends passing beyond the wood and the sound of boots and kit tinkling/clanking as the soldiers pass.

Ain Mudlarks. Late up, like us.

*There's a distant shout of 'Fucking tank!' The singing
stops, followed by three metallic booms as someone
bangs their rifle on its side. A cheer goes round the
company and they move on. The song continues as
their voices disappear.*

Voices Singing
Rolling on ... rolling on ... rolling on ... rolling on ...
By the light of the silvery moon,
Rolling on ... rolling on ... rolling on ... rolling on ...

*The crew waits until the voices have disappeared.
Then wait for Venus who is the last one back in the
circle, still with the die in his hand. He hands the die
back to Dice who catches it as if he was ready for it,
and puts it in his pocket.*
After a silence ...

Dice Now me belly starting to bad.

*Everyone looks to Child, who waits for a while,
before checking his watches.*

Child The Contour will be here soon. Let's be ready.

*Everyone starts to move, some clearing away their
equipment, and rolling blankets/groundsheets, etc.,
others scribbling letters. Ain starts to unhook the
blankets around the room, revealing the woman
asleep inside. She wakes.*

Ain Last call for Love Lane ... ?

*He looks at Lion and Dice, who both hesitate. Dice
nods Lion on.*

Lion Moment ... moment ...

*He goes inside and Ain hooks up the blanket again.
While this is happening Child goes across to
Kirkpatrick, unties him and takes off his mask.*

Kirkpatrick, sweating and panting, takes a few moments to recover.

Child Now you be honest. Tell us why you're here.

Kirkpatrick hesitates. Child goes to replace the mask.

You want this back on?

Kirkpatrick No . . . ! No . . .

Child So?

After a moment.

Kirkpatrick I overheard another crew talking after Poelcapelle.

Child What did you hear?

Kirkpatrick They said . . . they said there was a crew gone 'fanti', that's the word they used. A mixed race crew . . . that kept 'trophies'. Is it true?

Child From what you've seen of us, do you think we're savages?

Kirkpatrick Is it true?

Child takes his bag and brings out a small box. Everyone stops still to watch.

What's that?

Child hands it to Kirkpatrick, who looks inside, with trepidation.

Child Take it out.

Kirkpatrick brings out something wrapped in a cloth.

Open it.

Kirkpatrick slowly unwraps the cloth, until he sees what's inside.

Kirkpatrick Oh Christ!

He drops it. Everyone watching laughs and resumes what they were doing. Child picks up what has fallen and puts it back in the cloth.

What is it?

Child A souvenir, from Flers. We got stuck half way over and didn't recover our machine till the following year. We found the finger in our tracks. It was mummified like this when we found it.

Kirkpatrick's face shows utter disgust. Everyone laughs.

You didn't see the ring. That's rather the point . . .

He shows the ring. Kirkpatrick looks at it with revulsion.

Kirkpatrick 'Erin . . . Erim'? It's in German.

Child Yes. It's a German finger.

Kirkpatrick What does it say?

Child Zur erinnerung.

Kirkpatrick looks blank.

Remember me. Remember me. (*He starts carefully to rewrap it.*) This the sort of thing you were after?

Kirkpatrick I guess so . . .

Child He would have been a Holsteiner, you know. They occupied that stretch of the line. So, not German at all really, Danish. 'Remember me!' The Finger Prince of Denmark? Never mind. When you come to write your moral-shocker I don't suppose you'll bother to say we held it in respect? No. What would be the top-line? Either heroes or savages, eh?

Ain Oy . . . chief, you're not gonna go into one are you?

Child Absolutely not. (*searching in his knapsack*) Who had my book?

Mo takes out the book and hands it to Child.

Mo Me. We never got to the last one . . .

Child flicks to the last poem and smiles. He is about to put it into his knapsack but thinks better of it and hands it to Kirkpatrick. (In Child's edition the last poem is 'The Voice of the Ancient Bard'.)

Child Here. I won't read it again. Take these . . . (*handing him letters*)

Lion comes out of the room, buttoning himself up.

Where's Dice?

Ain Picking a daisy.

Child I want you packed up quick. (*at the letter-writers*) Finish. (*at the hung blankets*) Take it down. I want five minutes. Five minutes.

He takes a moment to finish a letter, as Dice returns.

Move your fat brown arse.

Dice I just moved it big time, mass.

Child On the jildi!

Venus and Duff rapidly seal their envelopes and give them to Kirkpatrick as the woman emerges from the dismantled room, to sit, waiting.

(*at the dixie of tea*) Leave a cupful for the Contour. (*nodding at Kirkpatrick and the woman*) And two lights for them.

Cossum takes a cupful out of the dixie and pours the rest away.

Ain We need some sugar for the lady.

Everyone comes forward with money.

Duff (*with a note*) That's all I got.

Child You taking it with you?

Ain I only got dust . . .

Dice Me too, jus' a whole heap o'shrapnel . . .

Child Don't vex, we're over.

He gives it to her. She proceeds to count it. Child then seals the letter he has been writing and hands it to Kirkpatrick.

Here.

Everyone gathers together, some standing, others sitting or crouching.

(*to Lion*) Take it on.

Lion I won't say a prayer, we're spread too wide for a prayer . . . but if any one has any wise words, anything, from memory or in your heart, for yourself or another, say it out.

After a silence.

I know only that death is real, and everything else that appears is unreal.

Silence.

That a drop of water that falls in the ocean all can perceive. That the drop and the ocean are one, few can comprehend.

Silence.

Mo I am poured out like water . . . and all my bones are out of joint . . . my heart is wax . . . it is melted inside me . . . my tongue sticks to my mouth. A man can conceal himself from his enemies, not from his friends.

Silence.

Cossum Greater love hath no man than – than – than . . . that he lay down his life for his friends.

Silence.

Dice To everything there is a season, and a time to every purpose under the heaven. A time to be born and a time to die, a time to kill and a time to heal, a time to mourn and a time to dance, a time to embrace and a time to refrain, a time to keep silence and a time to speak, a time to love and time to hate, a time of war and a time of peace.

Ain We are made of yesterdays, and know nothing, because our days upon earth are a shadow . . . for . . . for . . . (*struggling to remember the end of the sentence*)

Venus . . . for a thousand years are but a yesterday, and all our days are but a tale to be told.

Silence.

Child Yesterday is past, our today is our future, our tomorrow is secret.

Silence. Some wait for Duff.

Duff (*after a while*) A rat cannot go into its hole if there's a winnowing-fan tied to its belly.

Several (*beat*) What/Eh?!

Duff shrugs.
    Everyone cracks up, including Dice. Duff is silently pleased with himself.

Reconnaissance Officer (*quietly*) Good evening, gentlemen.

*Everyone freezes, turning to see the figure of the
Reconnaissance Officer watching them from the
shadows. He wears the hood of his parka up,
concealing his face, and carries maps, and a
contraption with wires and lights over one shoulder.*

Child Our ferryman. Silent as ever.

Reconnaissance Officer It's a talent.

Child (*checking his watches*) . . . And bang on time.

Reconnaissance Officer Where's your machine?

Child Edge of the wood.

*The Reconnaissance Officer steps into the light,
revealing himself to be a middle-aged man, with a
very battle-hardened face. He hands Child a map
rolled up in a tube. Child spreads it on the ground.
The others gather to look at the map, concerned.*

Reconnaissance Officer What was wrong with it?

Ain Fuel feed. Fixed now.

*The Reconnaissance Officer is staring at Kirkpatrick
and the woman.*

Reconnaissance Officer Tourists?

Ain American.

They look at the photograph over Child's shoulder.

Kirkpatrick Good evening, sir . . .

Reconnaissance Officer (*completely ignoring him*) It's
two days old. (*indicating the photo*) Your starting point.
Their FL . . . three hundred and twenty yards. Wire.
Flattish. Three holes straight in front, there, here, here,
all sheer. Rest uneven, hard to read.

Child is taking measurements with an angle compass and ruler, saying them to Mo who is jotting them down and making calculations with a small slide-rule.

Child (*to Mo*) Forward thirty . . . left forty-five . . . forward thirty, thirty-five, forty . . . right ninety . . . forward twenty . . . left forty-five . . . on.

Mo Forward thirty . . . left forty-five . . . forward thirty-five? . . .

Child Forty.

Mo Forty . . . right ninety . . . forward twenty . . . left forty-five . . . on.

A cup of tea is handed to the Reconnaissance Officer.

Child Arcs from the off.

Mo Firing blind?

Child What the fuck, eh? Let's start open and stay open.

The gunners take down their arcs of fire as Mo calls them.

Mo Joe . . . open tight . . . port, close, starboard three-one-five to three-sixty . . . port, narrow to three-forty. Singsong . . .

Lion Open, zero to twenty-five, port, open zero to sixty, starboard narrow to ten, port, open, zero forty-five.

Mo finishes the calculation.

Mo Very good. Coss . . . Twenty to forty-five, port, fifty-five one-two-five, starboard, close, port, open forty wide.

Ain Right, let's drill it, while we've got some light. No mistakes, lads.

They form up into a bunch with lanterns, in their rough operational positions, some crouching, some

standing: Child and Ain at the front, Venus in front
of Mo on the left side (audience's right), Lion in front
of Cossum on the right side (audience's left), Duff
and Dice standing far and near behind, perhaps
blindfolding their eyes.

Child Ready?

He takes a deep breath and starts . . .
   As they go through the operation, everyone
concentrates hard on their pieces of paper rather than
doing any actions. The sequence is led by Child, with
map and wristwatches, who counts each forward
movement in yards, beginning at a second to each
yard and getting quicker, and the turns, calling port
or starboard and giving sign gestures and taps on
the shoulder to Ain next to him. Ain in turn, signs
and calls each gear change to Duff and Dice behind,
who pace back and forward at each call ('Up . . .
up . . . up . . . up . . . free! . . . stop port . . . free
port . . . up . . . up . . . up . . . up', etc.). They call
back, 'Done . . . done . . . done . . . done . . . free . . .
done . . . ', etc. Child in addition calls the brakes that
he operates ('Brakes . . . release . . . brakes . . . ', etc.).
The four gunners call 'open' and 'close', 'narrow' and
'wide' with their numbers respectively as they open
their guns and change their arcs of fire. The sequence
should take no longer than a minute. Its awesomeness
should not be in its noise (everyone makes their calls
in concentrated low voices), but in the astonishing
synchronicity.
   After the last port turn, rising to highest gear, and
the following calls from all members . . . everyone
should stop almost in unison. There should be a
silence.

Child . . . Green fields.

Reconnaissance Officer Ready to roll?

Everyone starts to collect their kit.

Child Any noise cover laid on?

The Reconnaissance Officer slings his tea and puts the lights on his back.

Reconnaissance Officer Won't need it. Wind's from the north-east, just keep her in low, usual routine. I'll take it slow. Follow me at twenty yards. If I can I'll flash a green before a stop. (*He does so.*) Do you want a minute?

Child looks round at his crew and nods.

I'll be ahead.

The Reconnaissance Officer moves off towards the tank. They watch him go, and gather nervously.

Child Once we move from here, silence, eh. Don't waste this now.

The crew wait apprehensively, Mo attaching facemail.

Venus Ey . . . who stinks?

Cossum Me. I've got a muck-sweat on like a pig.

Duff I can't roll this . . . (*at his cigarette*)

Venus gives him one from a packet.

Ain Okay. Let's tighten up.

Duff curses, shaking too much to light it. Venus lights it for him.

Let's get up for it now . . . you there? You there?

Several nod. Lion has been trying to spit on the ground.

Lion Fuck drymouth.

Mo (*very quiet*) I'm not there.

Child What?

Mo just shakes his head.

Mo I'm not ready's what.

Everyone exchanges uneasy looks. Mo attaches the facemail round his face to cover it from the others.

Ain Come on, matey, one last time. Green fields, Mo, green fields. Say it over, in your head . . .

Mo Green fields green fields green fields . . .

Child That's it, get up . . .

Mo I don't believe in Heaven.

Ain Take your time, take your time . . .

Mo simply shakes his head, in utter misery.

(*to Dice*) Make us rhyme.

After a moment of gathering his thoughts . . .

Dice Ice . . . ice . . . Now we ice . . . (*summoning a rhyme*)

Heart of ice . . .
Skin of steel . . .
Don't fret . . .
Don't feel . . .

Ain (*at Mo*) Take a breath . . .

Child That's it, that's it . . .

Dice Shut out death . . .

Lion Shut out your mind . . .

Dice See blind . . .

Child No thought . . .
   No fear . . .

Ain (*to Mo*) We're here . . .

Dice Death is short . . .

*Mo weeps silently, shaking. The others look at each
other to continue . . .*

Ain Let it go now . . . Let it go . . .

Lion You are strong . . .

Duff You're not alone . . .

Dice Eight or one . . .

Venus One heart . . .

Dice Never 'part . . .

Duff Life's a joke, Mo . . .

Lion Death is sleep . . .

Dice Till day peep . . . till sun poke.

Ain You're with us Mo . . .

Dice We late. We late . . .

Ain Let's go, mate.

   Beat.

Through the red . . .

Dice Through the colours . . . Living dead . . .

Child Keep our bond . . .

Dice Sshh. All said.

Ain From mud . . .

Several . . . through blood . . .

All Seven . . . to the green fields beyond.

All Eight
To the green fields beyond.
To the green fields beyond.

They shoulder their packs and go.
  Kirkpatrick and the woman watch them disappear.
When they have gone he takes a pull from his flask
and looks at the letters. Taking out a pocket-knife he
slices one open. He glances through it and replaces it.
Opening another, he sees the woman giving him a
hard stare.

Kirkpatrick I'll send them on! There's a lot of Tommies
with strange ideas . . . (*He makes a gesture to indicate*
madness.) People up there keen to know. Don't judge
me. This is my work. (*He frowns at the second letter.*
Reading)
  'Dear Sir . . . Since you are reading our letters I thought
I would leave you something directly . . . ' (*He reacts.*)
  'Perhaps I have the "image" you are searching for.
When we came to France, we used to train, before we
had a tank, running round a field tied together in an iron
hoop. It was at Achincourt. On the same field fought
over five hundred years ago by armoured knights of old.
What *are* we, a tank crew, but eight pieces of a knight?
What if we are not made of dust, but something not
entirely of this world? What does it mean for a soul to
live out of its time? To live before it lives?
  'Before you dip your pen into the ocean of this war
remember . . . there are more things in it than are dreamt
of in any History.' (*He looks up and sees the woman still*
waiting.) It's gone cold. (*He puts the letters away, picks*
up his lantern, and goes.)

SIX

As the woman packs away her things to follow him, a figure walks slowly towards the clearing. It is a moment before we recognise Ain. He is dressed in a chauffeur's uniform from 1919. The woman is invisible to him, and he to her.

As he arrives and stops in the clearing she leaves towards the car and Kirkpatrick.

Ain looks around at the wood and the clearing, takes off his cap and sits, lighting a cigarette.

Ain (*to the audience directly*) I woke up. I was sitting against the side of the machine. The air felt fresh. She was burning. Everything was going off. My legs were on fire. I rolled over in the mud. There was a man there with a bayonet. I grabbed it. It went into my arm. I got hit on the side of the head. I woke up. I was lying in the bottom of a trench. There were ten or twenty faces staring at me. They were angry. Each man got to his feet and kicked me. I understood. I woke up. Another trench. Two men were hitting me. Taking it in turns with a block of wood. I woke up. I was being pushed, down trenches. I kept falling. I passed through men waiting on each side, as I went they spat and kicked me. I took my band off. I got blown against the parados. I woke up. I was in a dug-out. Three men sat in candle-light. They asked me questions. I couldn't answer. They put me in a hole dug in the wall. I remember thinking clearly I'm not dead. I remember thinking, it seemed so clear, I'm not dead because I'm dead. I'm not dead because I'm dead. There could never be no other explanation. I knew my mind had led me to another place, that's where I was. I was in the hole three days. When the pain came back it all became confused again, and I started having visions . . .

Cossum's Voice (*close by*) Else, mate. Else, mate! Where are you?

Ain I'm here. Where are you?

Cossum appears from behind the trees.

Cossum Fucked if I know.

Ain (*seeing someone else in the darkness*) Is that you? Chief?

Dice appears from the shadows as Cossum sits quietly by the fire.

Dice Yes.

Ain You're alive!? What happened to you? You were hit . . . you were in pieces . . .

Dice You'll laugh . . .

Ain I won't, I won't . . .

Dice I gathered myself up.

Ain Did it hurt?

Venus What do you think?

Dice joins Cossum around the fire.

Ain Where *are* you?

Mo suddenly appears, on his other side.

Mo It has a hundred names . . .

Duff appears, as Mo joins the others at the fire.

Duff You're only dreaming . . . (*He sits with the others.*)

Ain How can I be?

Lion walks out from the trees with a log for the fire.

Lion (*mimicking him*) 'How can he be! How can he be!'

Child is already sitting with the others by the fire.

Child Everything is absolutely true. Just some things more than others.

Lion puts a log on the fire, it bursts into flames. All seven are now around the fire, as at some time in the past, very relaxed, sitting, eating and watching the flames. Ain is sitting both outside the group and yet a part of it, as if it is half-memory, half-present.
After a silence . . .

Venus (*saying the word with a silly voice*) War!

Everyone starts giggling. It's a while before they settle down again.

Mo (*also playing with its sound*) Woooooooor!

Again all laugh, and settle.

Duff (*as if randily at a woman*) Whoo-ooah!

All crack up . . .

Dice Wah! (*with a pelvic thrust*)

Everyone continues in hysterics. Settling again.

Child (*very pompously, as if a declaration of hostilities*) WAR!

Everyone in hysterics once more. Settling again.

Cossum (*as a mad West-Countryman, with rolling eyes*) Warrr!

Laughter again, and silence.

Lion (*as a bemused caricature Hindu*) War?

Everyone completely collapses in helpless laughter. When it eventually subsides the focus turns to Ain.

*He looks up at the sky, with eyes closed, and utters
more a breath than a word, as if suddenly taken away
by a thought or a memory . . .*

Ain Wa . . .

He touches the ground.

Fade/blackout.

Glossary

APB   armour-piercing bullet
babbling   cooking (Cockney rhyming slang)
Babu   Jamaican slang for Asian (here jocular)
belly   get stranded, unable to move (tank technical term)
Black Marias   heavy high-explosive shells
black up   get upset, agitated
bobbing drill   target practice
bogeypoke!   'Fooled you!'
bonzer   jolly, easy, good (Australian army, from French)
breeze   fear
buckles   Jews (Cockney rhyming slang: buckle-my-shoes)
Bung   cheese
cacking   shitting
chub it   shut up
cod   fool
Contour   Reconnaissance Officer
crumped   broken, shell-holed
cuthberts   shirkers, slackers
dis   disconnected, wild (military term, literally 'detached from unit')
divvy   sharing-out duty
dobbs   pork
domplings   tits
doolally-tap   crazy (Indian army, after the military hospital in India)
duckboard glide   smooth, easy journey
duppy   zombie
dust   small change (coppers)
Emma-Gees   Machine-Gun Corps (MGs)

enfiladying for 'enfilading', military term for getting
  sideways to the enemy
'erb idiot (friendly)
fairy lights Very lights (after their inventor), night flares
fanti berserk, crazy, wild (Indian army)
farad forward, aggressive
fene be sick
flabadash hasty, slapdash
French Lady ghost (literally, someone who looks
  detached)
ghoul war reporter
H.E. high explosive
hate shellfire (military term)
Holy Friar . . . rax you, compree? This section translates
  literally as ' . . . a liar (Cockney rhyming slang: bad-
  intentioned, piss-taker). There's something not right
  about you, deceitful, evasive, 'wrong' about the way
  you talk. So don't trouble me any more, man of no
  faith, be honest, don't try to trick me or entrap me,
  or I'll get nasty, right?'
iniquity unease
Japan bread (from French, *du pain*)
jildi hasty, hastily (Indian)
kiff all right, calm
kinch easy, no problem
landowners/squires of the six-by-two the dead
licking-match fight
long out stick out
Lord Lovells shovels (Cockney rhyming slang)
mash-flat full speed
metal courage
morbs fear of death
mudlarks engineers
muuna vagina
mystery sausage
nanny granny

nation   race, own people
naughty   prostitute
needle   syphilis
nock   prostitute
nocturne   prostitute
novies   new members (pronounced 'novvies')
obbos   observation balloons
old pot   friend, old man (Cockney rhyming slang: 'old pot and pan')
onks   francs
open pack   get it all out in the open
out of curl   out of sorts, behaving oddly
peas   burning, hot (Cockney rhyming slang: 'peas-in-a-pot')
ponks   smells
rabbit pie, nifty   prostitute
rake   trick, try
rhymin'   making sense, talking sweetly
riddle   see through, suss
san fairy ann   nothing, it doesn't matter (from French, ça ne fait rien)
sheg   shag, intercourse
slingers   sausages
sponson   technical term for side-pods housing the tank's guns
sugar   money, cash
tab   ear
umptyiddies   nerves
Wha' brok?   'What happened? What have I missed?'
Wha' mek?   'What's up?'
whiff o' stiff   smell of human flesh/corpse
winnick   off one's head, crazy